KIDS' WIT

KIDS' WIT

Illustrations © Shutterstock
Additional illustrations by Isla and Carina McKay, Milla Roelofse and Elizabeth Clouting

Summersdale Publishers Ltd
46 West Street
Chichester
West Sussex
PO19 1RP
UK

www.summersdale.com

Printed and bound by CPI Group (UK) Ltd, Croydon, CR0 4YY

ISBN: 978-1-84953-651-6

Substantial discounts on bulk quantities of Summersdale books are available to corporations, professional associations and other organisations. For details contact Nicky Douglas by telephone: +44 (0) 1243 756902, fax: +44 (0) 1243 786300 or email: nicky@summersdale.com.

KIDS' WIT

the funniest things that children say

My granny is the oldest person in the WORLD!

Richard Benson

summersdale

Contents

Introduction

Anyone who has ever been around kids knows that out of the mouths of babes come the most hilarious statements. Whether it's a simple slip of the tongue, an innocent double entendre, a marvellous malapropism or just a minor mispronunciation, there's no doubt that the results of these mini mistakes have the ability to make you laugh out loud.

The beauty of these slip-ups is how blissfully unaware the perpetrators are, but sometimes their observations on the world can make you look at life with fresh eyes. From their profound philosophies to their hilarious, charming mistakes, this collection of the best baby bloopers will entertain, surprise and delight you.

Home Time

Parent:

Alright, bedtime.

Child:

OK, off to the land of Nob for me...

Helping Dad at the allotment:

Hoes are great, aren't they Daddy?
How many hoes do you have?

Parent:

The living room is such a tip!

Child:

It's OK, just wait until the morning –
it's always tidy then!

Parent:

Did you hit your brother?

Child:

No. Not yet.

Child:

I wish I was a squirrel.

Parent:

Why's that?

Child:

So I could eat lots of nuts.

Child:

What's wrong with Mummy?

Dad:

She's just feeling a bit blue.

Child:

Why doesn't she paint herself
another colour?

Parent:

Are you going to tidy your room?

Child:

Don't worry, I have it all under a troll.

After taking away his toys:

Mummy, I love you but I
just don't like you right now.

Mum:

That's not very nice, say 'sorry'.

Child (looking at the floor):

Sorry.

Mum:

No, say sorry to my face.

Child:

Sorry face.

Mummy, it's really sunny, can we go to the biatch?

Parent:

Where did you get those beautiful eyes?

Child:

From my face.

Daddy, what did you do before you met me?

It's a good thing I don't squeeze the dog as hard as I could, or he'd go bang!

Sister:

Mummy says that my freckles are the marks of angels' kisses.

Brother:

Mummy said to me that angels eat poo for breakfast.

Parent:

Behave!

Child:

I'm being haive!

Mummy, you have such pretty eyes.
I love all the pink lines on them.

Playing with his fire truck toy:

I love to play with my tire fuck.

**Don't drink all of the wine, Mummy —
save some for Daddy!**

Walking up the stairs to bed:

We really need to get an escalator in
the house. I can't just keep walking up
these stairs all the time.

Parent:

I think the dog's a little poorly.

Child:

Oh no, we'll have to take him
to the vegetarian!

Parent:

Do you love me?

Child:

Yes, but not as much as chicken.

Looking out of the window at the mist:

Look, it's gone all froggy outside!

Watching his mum change his sister's nappy:

Mummy, where has her willy gone?

Picking up their potty with wee and poo in it to show their parent:

Look, a swimming pool!

Child:

Are you going out for dinner?

Parent:

Yes, we're off to my friend's house.

Child:

What's their name?

Parent:

Emily.

Child:

Is he a girl, a boy or a bear?

Child:

Where does food go
when you eat it?

Parent:

It goes down your throat
and into your stomach.

Child:

And then does it go
into your legs?

And then they got married and lived politely ever after.

Parent:

You're not allowed to kick your brother in the head!

Child:

Where am I allowed to kick him then?

Daddy, my poo is coming, it's getting ready to dive!

Child:

What are you reading?

Parent:

It's a book called *The Hitchhiker's Guide to the Galaxy*. Do you want to see a picture of the author?

Child:

Is it an alien?

Growing Up

You can't use swear words
until you're thirty-six!

Parent:

We're going to arrange a nice funeral
service to say goodbye to Granny, and
we're going to bury her body in the
ground where it will be safe.

Child:

What about her head?

Child:

My fivehead hurts.

Parent:

You mean your forehead, sweetie.

Child:

No, I'm five now!

When I grow up I want to be a liar like Daddy.

Parent:

What do you want to be
when you grow up?

Child:

I think I will be a teacher.

Parent:

And what would you
like to teach?

Child:

Children, obviously!

Parent:

Come on now, clear up your toys –
you're nearly four now.

Child:

I don't have to, I'm still three!

Mum:

What do you want to be
when you grow up?

Child:

A duck.

To Grandma:

Why is your face so creased –
did you shut it in the door?

To Grandad:

Are you all wrinkly because you spent
so long in the bath this morning?

This is my grandma.
She's old and is going to die soon.

When I get bigger, I want to
play rugby and be a scum
half like Daddy!

Mummy, I can't grow up to
be a puppy, can I?

After a programme finishes on TV:

Oh no, if it's MORE *Dora the Explorer* I'm going to DIE!

My granny is the oldest
person in the WORLD!

Child:

Granny, why are your eyes
so wrinkly?

Granny:

They're laughter lines –
you'll get them one day.

Child:

Really? You must have heard
some really funny jokes.

I don't like being six, it's the oldest I've ever been.

Grandchild:

How old are you?

Grandparent:

I'm sixty-five years old.

Grandchild:

Did you start at one?

I'm four but my willy is still three!

Mum, do you put make-up on to stop you looking old?

What happens when you die? Is it like ice cream and you just melt away?

You don't look old yet – your face is still straight!

Parent:

What colour are your eyes?

Child:

Green.

Parent:

What colour are my eyes?

Child:

Blue.

Parent:

What colour are grandma's eyes?

Child:

Old.

Parent:

How does it feel to be
six, sweetie?

Child:

You know how it feels to be
six, you were six two
hundred years ago!

Three-year-old:

Mummy, you need to stop calling me a child!

Mum:

But you are a child!

Three-year-old:

I'm not a child any more, I'm a toddler!

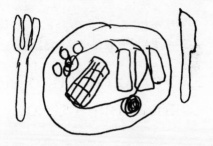

Dinner Time

We are being green and eating only orgasmic vegetables.

Parent:

Would you like to try some almond milk?

Child:

Is that what baby almonds drink?

I need a fock to help my knife.

Parent:

Do you want any pudding?

Child:

No! I don't want pudding,
all I need is football.

My favourite type of food is
ornamental food.

On the way to McDonalds:

Parent:

Behave yourself or you won't get a Happy Meal.

Child:

Will they give me a Sad Meal?

Parent:

Where do we get cold milk from?

Child:

From a cold cow.

Mum:

Could you wash your hands for dinner?

Child:

I washed them yesterday so they're nice and clean!

Could I have some wrench dressing for my salad?

Looking through a pack of Animal Crackers:

It says not to open if the seal is broken, but I can't find the seal!

Please can we have corn on the knob for dinner?

Eating an ice lolly:

It's cold all the way up to the moon!

Parent:

Did you enjoy dinner? I made it from scratch.

Child:

Who's Scratch?!

Parent:

Eat your greens, please.

Child:

No thank you, my taste bugs don't like them.

Can we have meatballs and marijuana sauce for dinner please?

In a posh restaurant:

Parent:

Make sure you eat all of your peas.

Child:

I've had enough now, I'll leave them for the waster.

No, Daddy, cans go in the cycling bin!

Parent:

What would you like to eat from the Chinese, dear?

Child:

I would like a romantic duck, please.

Long ago, did you have food?

Refusing to drink his milk:

NO! You're trying to put me to sleep!

You shouldn't put so much tobacco sauce on your food or you'll get cancer. We learnt about it at school.

Mum:

What should we make Daddy
for breakfast today?

Child:

Chips and beans and chips!

Parent:

Would you like a nice cold drink of water?

Child:

No, I prefer worm water.

Sisi took my sausage! Tell her to stop being shellfish!

Child:

Can I have ice cream?

Parent:

Maybe later.

Child (waits ten seconds):

Is it later yet?

Parent:

There's a punnet of
strawberries in the fridge.

Child:

We learnt about punnets the
other day in school! Why did
you put a poem in the fridge?

After a coughing fit:

My tongue is drowning!

Trying to open a bottle of medicine:

Mother:

You can't open that — it has a childproof cap.

Child:

How does it know it's me?

Stepping onto the bathroom scales:

How much do I cost?

Out and About

Child:

I wish I could roller skate.

Parent:

Why can't you?

Child:

Because it takes three months to learn and you need really flexible feet.

Child:

I spy with my little eye,
something beginning with 'o'.

Parent:

Orange?

Child:

No silly, something outside the
car.

Parent:

I'm going to have to give up.

Child:

'Orse! Over there in the field!

While clothes shopping with her mother:

Mummy, why do my clothes always have to match? Yours don't.

Mummy and Daddy took me out on the lake today in a dingy.

On seeing a teacher in the supermarket:

Mrs Foster, what are you doing here?! You live at school!

After falling off her bike:

Ow! My crouch hurts!

Can we go to the zoo again soon?
I want to see the kangaroos
and little wallies!

Seeing someone mowing the lawn:

I didn't realise grass has its
hair cut too.

In a supermarket, on noticing that his nappy is beginning to sag:

Daddy, my bottom's hanging off!

At the swimming pool:

How does that rope stop the deep water from going in the shallow water?

Parent:

Leave your crisps in the car and save them for when we get back.

Child:

No. We will stay in the car until I have finished them all. Then we can get out.

On seeing an overweight man in the supermarket, in what is intended to be a whisper:

Is that man having a baby?

Telling a friend about a play he saw at the weekend:

And it was so good they all gave
it a standing ovulation!

Waiting to board a flight at the airport, on seeing the pilot and co-pilot arrive:

Look Mummy, it's the pirates!

After playing in the pool for an hour:

Mummy, look — I'm all wrinkly. I
look like granddad!

Child:

How deep is the water
in the pool, Daddy?

Dad:

About six feet deep.

Child:

Are those your feet or
my feet, Daddy?

Parent:

When crossing the road,
what do we listen for?

Child:

Snakes?

After running around the park:

My heart is beeping so fast!

Driving past a sign for a 'Ladies' Warehouse':

Let's go to the Ladies' Whorehouse!

Aunt:

I'd like you to be the ring bearer
at my wedding.

Nephew:

Do I have to wear a bear
costume and roar lots?

*Watching a play where the
actors are dressed in
animal costumes:*

Daddy, why can't our dog speak like that one?

On seeing a field of cows:

Child:

Mummy, how do you tell which cows
will produce which milk?

Mum:

I'm sorry, what do you mean?

Child:

Well, which ones produce red top and
which ones produce green top?

Parent:

Can you hear the bird
singing?

Child:

Yes, but I can't see it. Is it a
see-through bird?!

*Passing a sign that
says 'hidden drive':*

It's not much of a secret any
more if they tell you!

School Time

Teacher:

Who helps you with your homework?

Child:

My Daddy teaches me meth and my Mummy helps me with English.

Teacher:

What shapes can you name?

Kid:

Circle... square... rectal...

Teacher:

Can you spell your
mum's name?

First child:

Yes, it's M-U-M!

Second child:

That's funny, that's my
mum's name, too!

Looking forward to sports day:

I can't wait to see the obstacle horse!

I love *Matilda* because the main character is a very strong heron.

Teacher:

What do we call a long, long book with lots of words and no pictures?

Child:

A naval.

Gravity wants to get you. You just need to jump when it's not looking.

Child:

Miss, where's our usual teacher today?

Supply teacher:

She has a headache and has gone home for the day.

Child:

Perhaps she had too much to drink — that always gives my mum a headache.

The teacher said we should put up our hands if we need the toilet, but it doesn't help. I think she's lying.

Teacher:

Who wrote *Romeo and Juliet*?

Child:

Willy and Jack Spear.

We learned about birds today in class. We learned that owls go 'wooh wooh' and they are not turtle.

Teacher:

Why are you doing your maths
paper on the floor?

Child:

You told me I couldn't use tables.

Teacher:

How do birds keep warm in winter?

Child:

Do they have blankets?

Teacher:

What's the capital of Scotland?

Child:

S.

Teacher:

Can anyone name two types of whale?

Child:

A blue whale and a spunk whale.

Teacher:

Where does wood come from?

Child:

Trees.

Teacher:

And where does leather come from?

Child:

Tesco.

One way of looking after animals and their homes is being a wildlife conversationalist.

Teacher:

What do insects use their antennae for?

Child:

So they can watch TV?

Teacher:

Who was king before Charles the First?

Child:

No one, he was the first.

Teacher:

Why is July the fourth important
to Americans?

Child:

It's when they celebrate... Indie
Pan Dance Day?

Teacher:

What do the letters U–S–A stand for?

Child:

The United Stacks of America.

Teacher:

Why was the war of 1939 to 1945
called World War Two?

Child:

Because there had already been a world
war and this was a world war too.

Teacher:

What do we call the period of history
during which Leonardo da Vinci and
Michelangelo were working?

Child:

The Runny Sauce?

Teacher:

What sound do cows make?

Child:

Moo!

Teacher:

And what do we call a baby cow?

Child:

A moose!

I like school except for fizzies lessons.

Genghis Khan was a very powerful worrier.

Teacher:

Does anybody know what we call a giant wave that rushes onto land and can destroy whole towns?

Child:

A salami!

My favourite president was April Ham Lincoln because she had ham as her middle name.

My ancestors went over to America on the *Wallflower*!

Teacher:

As a citizen of Europe, what does that make you?

Child:

An astronaut?

We're going to learn about Ancient Grease at school next week. The grease in our oven is *really* ancient so I already know all about it.

The Birds and The Bees

When you love somebody, your eyelashes go up and down and little stars and rainbows come out of you.

Young child telling his mum how he got a girlfriend at school:

I told her she had to be my girlfriend or she'd never see her hamster again.

You can tell if two people are going out because they smell nice. If they're just wearing trainers they're probably not going out.

When you get married,
can I be the husher?

Mother:

You look upset, what's wrong?

Son:

Lucy won't be my girlfriend even
though I really really lick her.

My dad told me I need to ask someone's
permission before I kiss them, but I'm
allowed to kiss my mum whenever I like.

I wish I was a boy. Willies look much more fun to play with.

The 'F word' is a bit like sex, but you don't love the other person.

If you have a girlfriend you have to buy them flowers, otherwise they will get cross. But if you buy the flowers from a garage they will get even crosser.

> **When a woman marries a man she takes him to be her awful wedded husband.**

Child:

Mommy, you have a big fat belly.

Mum:

It's big because I'm pregnant, dear.

Child:

Mommy, you have a big fat pregnant belly!

A small child is with his teenage babysitter in the park, when they see two adults kissing:

Child:

What are they doing?

Babysitter:

They're French kissing. It's what grown-ups do.

Child:

But they don't look French!

Consoling her daughter after finding out her crush doesn't fancy her back:

Mum:

Don't worry, there are plenty more fish in the sea.

Daughter:

I'm not marrying a FISH!

Child sitting in a plastic toy car, pressing the horn:

Mum, look, I'm really horny!

Uncle:

Meet Sarah, she's my fianceé.

Child:

What's a fianceé?

Uncle:

It means we're going to get married.

Child:

Why would she want to marry you?

A Mum is telling a story about an incident a few years ago:

Child:

Where was I?

Mum:

Back then you were still in my tummy.

Child:

I have pasta in my tummy.

My mum says when you love someone very much you have to wear a poppadom.

Child:

Why is that lady so big?

Parent:

Because she's pregnant — there's a baby growing in her tummy.

Child:

Does she have a baby in her bottom, too?

Dressing Up

Mummy, you'd look much nicer if your skin fitted your neck.

Pants are like pillows, but for bums.

Have you seen my gloves? They are stripy, and they are shaped like my hand.

Mum:

Do you think that dress
would look nice on me?

Child:

No, it's too small.

Mum:

Well I could get it in a bigger size.

Child:

But you'd still be fat.

**Are you going to iron
daddy's shit today?**

Aunt:

Don't you look cute in your best clothes? I could just eat you up!

Child:

Aaaaaahhh!!! Please don't eat me!

Child:

Daddy, how did you afford to buy so many clothes?

Dad:

There was a sale, everything was half off.

Child:

Then where's the other half?

Pointing to a bald man with a beard:

Daddy, why has that man's hair slipped?

Remarking on her niece's new dress:

Aunt:

Oh wow, what are you wearing there?

Child (lifting her skirt):

Knickers!

Parent:

What would you like to be for Halloween?

Child:

I'd like to be a bloody man covered in blood that has a big knife with blood on it, and an eyepatch.

Parent:

Do you want to wear your jumpsuit today?

Child:

No Mummy, my legs are tired and I don't want to have to jump today.

Sunday School

Reading a Bible story to child:

Parent:

The man named Lot was warned to take his wife and flee out of the city, but his wife looked back and was turned to salt.

Child:

What happened to the flea?

Lead us not into temptation, but deliver us some email...

Did God mean for giraffes to look like that or was it an accident?

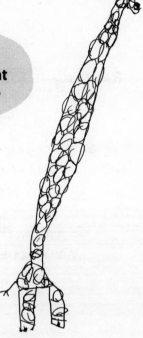

Dear God,
Thank you for my baby brother but I would have preferred a kitten.

Mummy, are you a
Catholic or a prostitute?

To get closer to enlightenment,
Buddhist monks spend lots
of time medicating.

When it rains, is God
crying or weeing?

Parent:

God is with us in this room, son.

Son:

Are you God?

Parent:

No, son.

Son:

Am I God?!

Parent:

You need to do your homework or you'll get in trouble.

Child:

You're not the boss of me! God's the boss of me and he says I don't need to do my homework!

Today, I learnt that the funny dresses that priests wear are called Cossacks.

The reverend says if I'm good my immoral soul will live forever in heaven.

Teacher:

Does anyone know what a Rabbi is?

Pupil:

Is it like a rabbit, only shorter?

What was Jesus' first name?

While walking home in a thunderstorm, a little child stops at every lightning flash:

Parent:

Why do you keep stopping – we need to rush home!

Child:

God's taking my photograph!

Teacher:

What's another name for Jesus?

Child:

Father Christmas?

Walking past a Scientology church:

That's where the people in white coats work on solar panels, isn't it Mum?

Teacher:

Can anyone tell me what brotherhood is?

Child:

Is it like Little Red Riding Hood?

After listening to carol singers singing 'Away in a Manger':

How does Wayne fit in a manger?

Child:

What did Jesus' dad do?

Teacher:

He was a carpenter. Do you know
what a carpenter does?

Child:

He lays carpets.

Child singing 'Lord of the Dance':

Dance, then, wherever you may be, I
am the Lord of the darts settee.

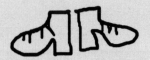

Teacher:

Tell me about heaven.

Child:

It's full of shoes.

Teacher:

Really, how come?

Child:

My mum says it's where
all the old soles go!

Curiouser and Curiouser

Child:

Do dinosaurs have lips?

Parent:

I don't think so.

Child:

So what do they lick?

Mummy, why is there a hole in your tights? Did a wolf bite you?

Seeing an adult's hairy legs:

Why have you got spiders on your legs?

If you kept hula hooping for ever, you'd fly away into the sun.

I like skipping. It's like making my feet clap.

Looking at the night sky:

Daddy, half the moon has broken off, where has it gone!

Does David Beckham pee?

After breaking wind in public, a small child shouts:

Oh, Mummy!

I had a fraction in my thumb!

On hearing a clap of thunder:

Why is the sky farting?

Child:

Daddy, will you change your shirt?

Dad:

Why? I've only just put this one on.

Child:

I'd love you more in a different shirt.

If you get a cut on your finger you should keep it clean or it will go sceptic.

On election day people draw an X next to who they want to vote for and put their vote in the ballet box.

Why don't goldfish sink?

Parent:

See you later, alligator!

Child:

In a while, paedophile!

I always want to be with you, Mummy. I wish I could cut off your head and carry it around with me all the time.

Mum:

Say sorry to your brother
for hitting him.

Child:

But I'm not sure I'm sorry.

Mum:

You should be sorry, and
you should say it anyway.

Child (to brother):

I'm pretty sure I'm sorry.

Mummy, I'm going to look after you to make sure no one steals you. If they do, we'll buy a new mummy.

Parent:

Adios amigo!

Child:

I'm sorry, I don't speak Spinach.

Dad:

Goodnight, son.

Son:

Goodbye, dad.

Dad:

No, it's goodnight.

Son:

Not this time it's not...

Dad:

You've got to use lots of elbow grease
to get the plates clean, you see!

Child:

Mummy said you should
use washing-up liquid.

Mum:

My jumper is a bit scratchy today.

Child:

Shall I get you some plasters
for the scratches?

Dinosaurs loved to skateboard, right Dad?

To his friend who is sleeping over:

Tell me when you're asleep, OK?

You're lucky to be alive, Mum.

Mum:

I wish you'd make up your mind!

Child:

How do I put make-up on my mind?

After running around the garden, a child is panting:

Parent:

Oh dear, are you out of breath?

Child:

No, I have more.

When you die, where do they put the cork?

Trying to copy Mum:

Would you just shit down!

Do rabbits speak Spanish?

Are ladies with hair on their legs really men?

After lots of snow:

Mummy, Mummy, there's a testicle hanging from the roof!

Mum:

Are you ticklish?

Child:

No, I'm English!

I saw a herd of cantaloupe at the weekend.

Mum, do you write about me in your diarrhoea?

My brother just yelled in my eye!

Watching his mum breastfeed his baby sister:

Mum, why have you got two of them?
Is one hot and one cold?

Child:

What's that, Dad?

Dad:

It's a tube of silicon for my DIY project.

Child:

A tube of skeletons for your die project?

After stepping on a pencil:

Oh no! I've killed a pencil!

Are dinosaurs microwaveable?

I can't poo — my bottom's asleep!

If you're interested in finding
out more about our books, find us on
Facebook at **Summersdale Publishers**
and follow us on Twitter at **@Summersdale**.

www.summersdale.com